Yellow Umbrella Books are published by Capstone Press
151 Good Counsel Drive, P.O. Box 669, Mankato, Minnesota 56002
http://www.capstone-press.com

1 2 3 4 5 6 07 06 05 04 03 02

Library of Congress Cataloging-in-Publication Data
Tucker, Shirley.
    Odd and even numbers/by Shirley Tucker and Jane Rambo.
    p. cm. — (Math)
    Includes index.
    Summary: Simple text and photographs introduce the properties of odd and even numbers.
    ISBN 0-7368-1286-5
    1. Numbers, Natural—Juvenile literature. 2. Arithmetic. [1. Numbers, Natural.] I. Rambo, Jane. II. Title. III. Series.
QA141.3 .T83 2002
513.2—dc21
                                                              2002016827

Editorial Credits
Susan Evento, Managing Editor/Product Development; Elizabeth Jaffe, Senior Editor; Charles Hunt, Designer; Kimberly Danger and Heidi Schoof, Photo Researchers
Photo Credits
Cover: Scott Campbell/International Stock; Title Page: Uniphoto; Page 2: David F. Clobes; Page 3: David F. Clobes (left and right); Page 4: Wally Eberhart/Visuals Unlimited (top left), Bruce Berg/Visuals Unlimited (top right), John Sohlden/Visuals Unlimited (bottom right), Unicorn Stock (bottom left); Page 5: Uniphoto (top left), William Palmer/Visuals Unlimited (top middle), Jeff Greenberg/Visuals Unlimited (top right), Cheryl A. Ertelt (bottom right), Mark S. Skalny/Visuals Unlimited (bottom left); Page 6: Larry Dunmire/Photo Network (top), M&D Long/Visuals Unlimited (bottom); Page 7: Anthony Mercieca/Root Resources (top left), Frank Armstrong/Photo Network (top right), Aneal Vohra/Unicorn Stock (bottom right), Dee Culleny/Visuals Unlimited (top left), Page 8: Frank Armstrong/Photo Network (top), Cheryl Ertelt (bottom), Page 9: Inga Spence/Visuals Unlimited (top left), Roger Cole/Visuals Unlimited (top right), R. Al Simpson/Visuals Unlimited (bottom right), Phyllis Kedl/Unicorn Stock (bottom left); Page 11: Tom McCarthy/Unicorn Stock; Page 12: Sunstar/International Stock; Page 13: Jeff Greenberg/Visuals Unlimited (top), Kent & Donna Dannen (bottom); Page 14: Jeff Daly/Visuals Unlimited (top), Jakub Jasinski/Visuals Unlimited; Page 15: Cheryl Ertelt (top and bottom), Page 16: Fritz Polking/Bruce Coleman

Odd and Even Numbers

By Jane Rambo and Dr.Shirley Tucker

Consulting Editor: Gail Saunders-Smith, Ph.D.

Consultants: Claudine Jellison and Patricia Williams,
ers
Cor Kaufman,
Math Learni ne Dalton School

Yellow Umbrella Books

an imprint of Capstone Press
Mankato, Minnesota

These are whole numbers.

1 3 5 7 9
0 2 4 6 8

We use these whole numbers
to write any whole numbers.

10 35 68 47
100 8 24 9

Whole numbers can belong to two different sets.

Odd Set:

1 3 5 7 9

Even Set:

0 2 4 6 8

The Even Set

0 2 4 6 8

Except for **0**, even numbers can be grouped into sets of **2**s, called pairs.

2 tulips

4 kittens

6 kids

8 eggs

The Odd Set

1 3 5 7 9

Except for **1**, odd numbers can be grouped in pairs with **1** left over.

1 duck

5 eggs

9 helmets

7 crayons

3 puppies

Here are **2** feet.

Here are **12** eggs.

These are even numbers.

Which numbers below are even numbers?

3 eggs

4 kids

2 kittens

1 puppy

A tricycle has **3** wheels.

Here are **5** sisters.

These are odd numbers.

Which numbers below are odd numbers?

4 tulips

3 apples

5 geese

3 swings

Here are whole numbers
on a number line.

0 1 2 3 4 5 6 7 8 9

Odd numbers are always
found between even numbers
on a number line.
To tell if numbers are even or
odd, look at the ones' place.

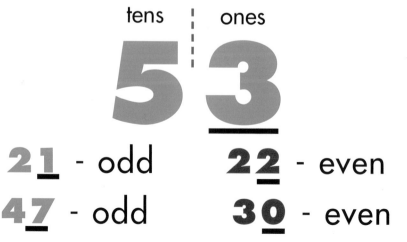

tens | ones
5 | 3

2<u>1</u> - odd   **2<u>2</u>** - even
4<u>7</u> - odd   **3<u>0</u>** - even

There are **13** students
in this class going to lunch.
Is **13** an even or odd number?
Look at the ones' place to
help you decide.

This class is in the park.
There are **12** students.

Is **12** an odd or even number?
Look at the ones' place
to help you decide.

Now let's see what happens
to odd and even numbers
when we add them.
If we add two even numbers,
we get an even number.

4 kids

+ 2 kids
——————
= 6 kids

If we add two odd numbers,
we get an even number.
Let's try it!

3 cherries

+ **1** cherry

= **4** cherries

If I add one even number
and one odd number,
is the sum even or odd?
Let's try it.

4 dogs

+ **3** dogs
_____

= **7** dogs

Every whole number is either odd or even.

If it's even, it is **0** or can be grouped into perfect sets of **2**s, called pairs.

If it's odd, it is **1** or can be grouped in pairs with **1** left over.

Words to Know/Index

add—to find the sum of two or more numbers; pages 13, 14, 15

belong—to be part of a group; page 3

decide—to choose or make up your mind about something; pages 11, 12

different—not the same; page 3

even—a number that can be put in pairs; pages 3, 4, 6, 7, 10, 11, 12, 13, 14, 15, 16

except—not a part of the group; pages 4, 5

group—things that go together; pages 4, 5, 16

number line—numbers put in order on a line to help you add and subtract; page 10

number set—a group of numbers that belong together; pages 2, 3, 4, 5

odd—a number that cannot be put in pairs without having one left over; pages 3, 5, 8, 9, 10, 11, 12, 13, 14, 15, 16

pair—two things that go together; pages 4, 5, 16

sum—the total you get when you put things together; page 15

whole number—any of the set of numbers that begins with zero and goes up by one; pages 2, 3, 10, 16

zero—empty or having no value; pages 2, 3, 4, 10, 16

Word Count: 286
Early-Intervention Level:12